Pure Pleasures

cupcake heaven.

raw food sweets
that make your
heart skip a beat

by Natalia KW

www.NataliaKW.com

Pure Pleasures cupcake heaven.

Food Styling and Photography by Natalia www.NataliaKW.com
Book Design by Adam Mills / Bottomless Design www.bottomlessdesign.com
Photo of Natalia by Jerah Coviello www.ecovogue365.com
Edited by Justin Karoway-Waterhouse

ISBN-10: 1463771576
ISBN-13: 978-1463771577

All of the information contained in this book is based on my personal experience. This book is not to be treated as or to take the place of medical advice from a qualified health care professional. In the case of serious illness, please seek professional assistance.

CONTENTS

Cupcakes, Oh My!

Sometimes you are fully blessed with divine inspiration. In my world, sometimes that inspiration comes in the form of cupcakes—raw vegan cupcakes to be exact. I thrive on creative projects and I'm constantly challenging myself to raise the bar when it comes to recipe development. I don't want to reinvent the wheel—I want to come up with innovative recipes that are unlike any other I have experienced before. I surround myself with scraps of paper covered in scratchy notes, written when a hint of inspiration floats in. One of these notes, that sat on my desk for about a year, said "coconut flour cakes". That's it. I hadn't really given it too much thought. In fact, I had never even bought coconut flour as it was just coming on the market as a replacement for gluten-free baking. The day I saw raw, organic coconut flour in an online catalog, I bought it—and it still sat on my shelf for months before I began to experiment. Then, one fateful night, I was hungry for dessert and it was way later than I should have been thinking about eating. My craving persisted and I started rifling around my refrigerator and cupboards. I found carrots, agave, spices and that lonely bag of coconut flour. I popped the ingredients into my food processor and whipped up a very simple carrot cake. I blended up a quick cashew frosting and my husband Adam and I sat down for a late night snack. Wow. We were both floored. The texture was divine—light, fluffy and more cake-like than we had ever experienced in a raw dessert. Most raw cakes are nut based and though delicious, I had never fulfilled that fluffy cake craving that seemed to coincide with every birthday party I attended. After indulging in every sweet bite on my plate, I giggled. I hadn't measured a single ingredient or written down any details of the recipe—a classic move when I'm hungry and want immediate nourishment.

There was something very special about this creation. If you know anything about my story, you know that special diets ruled my world for much of my early 20's. There were years without birthday cakes and no cake on my wedding day. Cakes are the epitome of celebration for me and while struggling with illness, it was difficult to watch others indulge while I politely declined the offering. Healing through live food nutrition and emotional cleansing is absolutely deserving of a celebratory cake. Though this culinary discovery may have happened a couple of years later, it is never too late for parties and cakes! Now I celebrate everyday!

In the months that followed, the real recipe development began. Carrot cake was a starting point, but I didn't want every cake and cupcake to be orange. Using apples as a moist, sweet base was the next, natural solution for me. They were neutral enough to complement even the simplest of flavors, like a classic vanilla. I had instant success with vanilla and chocolate and then began to experiment as other cravings appeared—lemon, blueberry and cinnamon swirl all made their way into my kitchen (and my mouth!). By the time I was ready to release *Pure Pleasures*, I decided that these coconut flour cakes deserved a section of their own to show just how special they are. After its release, I started getting more into cupcakes, loving that they are perfectly portioned out and how sweetly they could be decorated with fancy papers and frosting tools. At the time I was planning my *Pure Pleasures* launch party, I decided to showcase cupcakes and cocktails (okay, mock-tails) as the feature of the celebration. After all, it was like a birthday party, for my first book! When all was said and done, I was cupcake obsessed and so were my guests. Because I don't sit still for a second, I immediately began the developments for this book, as a companion to *Pure Pleasures*, showcasing the magical world of fluffy cupcakes topped with luscious frostings that will truly make your heart skip a beat.

The following recipes are at the top of my list when it comes to pure food pleasure and indulgence. I am ecstatic to be able to share this joy with you, because in my world, everyone deserves to visit cupcake heaven once in a while.

With love and wishes of bliss!

♡Natalia

Cupcake Kitchen Tips

Making and indulging in raw cupcakes is pretty simple and of course, very pleasurable. These helpful tips will have you rocking & rolling in no time.

1. **All of these recipes were developed using a 7-cup food processor** for the cake batter. Though you can use larger, anything smaller might give you a bit of trouble. If at any time your processor has trouble with the load or gets stuck, you can divide the mixture and process in a few batches. Then transfer all the batches into a large bowl and mix well. This may happen once in a while if your measurements have been a little off between wet and dry ingredients. Don't worry, there's always a solution!

2. **Coconut flour measurements** are always based on loosely packed cups.

3. **Apple measurements** are based on chopping the apples small enough so you can get a very accurate measurement without air pockets.

4. **Coconut oil and cacao butter measurements** are based on liquid form. If you need to melt either of these, you can place them in a bowl in your dehydrator at 115° or you can use a double boiler method with mildly hot (not boiling) water.

5. **Unless otherwise noted, each recipe will yield about one dozen** regular sized cupcakes or 30 mini cupcakes. Filled cupcakes make about 15 regular cupcakes. I love the minis—they are the perfect sweet bite! If you're in a time crunch, just make a cake instead. This will save you the time of pressing each individual cupcake into place.

6. **I love to use silicone cupcake liners** to form the perfect shape. If you can't get your hands on them, just use a traditional cupcake baking pan and paper cupcake liners.

7. **For the frostings,** you will do best with a high-powered blender for smooth, even consistency.

8. **Some frostings here are very thick and rich** and others are a bit lighter and creamier. I love them both! Cacao butter will usually yield a thicker result than coconut oil. If you find yourself preferring one texture over the other, you can mix and match, but keep in mind that the flavor of cacao butter will always give you that underlying hint of white chocolate.

9 **Make your cupcakes pretty!** Experiment with pastry bags and tips for picture perfect results. Gather a fun selection of paper cupcake liners to send them over the top!

10 **These cupcakes store perfectly in the freezer for weeks!** They are best served after thawing—either from the refrigerator or at room temperature. In the refrigerator, they are fresh for about three days, keeping in mind the fruit base.

11 **These recipes call for raw honey or agave.** I find that my body is happier when I feed it health boosting honey. If honey does not fit into your lifestyle, then by all means, use agave! I have interchanged them on many occasions and have had great results with both. In some cases, I use agave exclusively to meet certain texture requirements.

12 **Enjoy the process,** experiment with new flavors and experience what cupcake heaven is all about!

SHOPPING LIST

Just so you are completely prepared when a cupcake craving hits, here is an all-inclusive shopping list for creating the recipes in this book. This list is not to intimidate—some of these ingredients are only used once.

Please go organic! My stance is organic always—I'm standing up for my health, the health of the planet and the health of the farmers that are generously creating our food source. Resources for purchasing are available on page 60.

Fruits & Veggies
Apples (any sweet variety)
Bananas
Blueberries (fresh & dried)
Blackberries
Strawberries
Raspberries
Goji Berries (dried)
Golden Berries or Cranberries (dried)
Cherries
Peaches
Lemons
Limes
Oranges
Mangos
Carrots
Beets

Raw Pantry
Raw Coconut Flour
Raw Coconut Oil
Raw Cacao Nibs
Raw Cacao Powder
Raw Cacao Butter
Spirulina
Himalayan Salt
Raw Coconut Butter
Raw Shredded & Dried Coconut

Sweeteners
Raw Honey
Raw Agave Nectar

Herbs, Spices & Flavorings
Vanilla Beans (substitute 1 teaspoon
     extract per bean if necessary)
Cinnamon
Nutmeg
Turmeric
Chili Powder
Cayenne
Cardamom
Fresh Mint Leaves
Fresh Basil Leaves
Fresh Ginger
Dried Lavender
Dried Rose Petals
Vanilla Extract
Almond Extract
Peppermint Extract

Nuts & Seeds
Raw Cashews
Raw Macadamia Nuts
Raw Pecans
Raw Walnuts
Poppy Seeds
Chia Seeds

the recipes

Cinnamon Swirl Cupcakes
with Cream Cheese Frosting

My classic vanilla bean cupcake, swirled with sweet & spicy ribbons of cinnamon syrup. Topped off with thick cashew cream cheese frosting, and wow—this one gets rave reviews.

makes one dozen regular or 30 mini cupcakes

Cinnamon Swirl Cupcakes

3 cups peeled and chopped apples
1 tablespoon lemon juice
¾ cup raw honey or agave
½ cup raw coconut oil
seeds of 2 vanilla beans
2 teaspoons organic vanilla extract
pinch of salt
2 cups raw coconut flour
⅓ cup agave nectar
1 tablespoon cinnamon
pinch of Himalayan salt

Cream Cheese Frosting

2½ cups raw cashews, soaked for 2
    hours, drained/rinsed
½ cup raw honey or agave
6 tablespoons lemon juice
¼ cup pure water
seeds of one vanilla bean
⅛ teaspoon Himalayan salt
⅓ cup raw coconut oil

Cinnamon Swirl Cupcakes Place the chopped apples in your food processor fit with the S-blade and process until smooth. Immediately add the lemon juice and process to prevent browning. Add the honey or agave, coconut oil, vanilla bean, vanilla extract & salt and process again until well combined. Finally, add the coconut flour and process until completely combined. In a small bowl, whisk together the agave nectar, cinnamon and salt until smooth. To assemble the cupcakes, fill your liner ⅓ of the way with the cake mixture and press to form. For mini cupcakes, drizzle ¼ teaspoon of the cinnamon syrup over the top of the cupcake. For regular sized cupcakes, drizzle ½ teaspoon of cinnamon syrup. Top with more cake until the liner is now ⅔ of the way full. Drizzle another ¼ (or ½) teaspoon of cinnamon syrup onto the cupcake. Finally top the cupcakes with more of the cake mixture until the liners are completely full. Freeze for 2 hours to firm. Once solid, pop the cupcakes out of the liners and they're ready to be frosted.

Cream Cheese Frosting Place the cashews, honey or agave, lemon, water, vanilla and salt in a high-speed blender. Blend until very smooth. Add the coconut oil and blend again until just combined. Refrigerate the frosting for 2-4 hours to firm. Once the it has thickened, frost the cupcakes.

cupcake heaven.

Sweet Lime Cupcakes
with Blueberry Frosting

I love sweet and sour lime desserts and this cupcake is no exception. The smooth, creamy blueberry frosting that tops them is luscious enough to eat on its own like a pudding. Between the light lime green cake and the purple berry frosting, the bright colors are so much fun and make an impressive plate on the dessert table. Seriously, who needs food coloring with all of the hues that nature has to offer? Not me.

makes one dozen regular or 30 mini cupcakes

Sweet Lime Cupcakes

2½ cups peeled and chopped apples
½ cup lime juice
1 cup raw honey or agave
½ cup raw coconut oil
2 teaspoons lime zest
¼ teaspoon turmeric (for color)
½ teaspoon of your favorite mild
   green superfood powder (for color)
pinch of Himalayan salt
3 cups raw coconut flour

Blueberry Frosting

2½ cups raw cashews, soaked for 2
   hours, drained/rinsed
1 cup blueberries
½ cup raw honey or agave
¼ cup lemon juice
1 vanilla bean
pinch of Himalayan salt
⅓ cup raw coconut oil

Sweet Lime Cupcakes Place the chopped apples in your food processor fit with the S-blade and process until smooth. Immediately add the lime juice and process to prevent browning. Add the honey or agave, coconut oil, lime zest, turmeric, green powder & salt and process again until well combined. Finally, add the coconut flour and process until completely combined. Fill your cupcake liners to the top and press firmly to form their shape. Freeze for 2 hours to firm. Once solid, pop the cupcakes out of the liners and they're ready to be frosted.

Blueberry Frosting Place the cashews, blueberries, honey or agave, lemon, vanilla and salt in a high-speed blender. Blend until very smooth. Add the coconut oil and blend again until just combined. Refrigerate the frosting for 2-4 hours to firm. Once it has thickened, frost the cupcakes.

cupcake heaven.

CHOCOLATE CHIP CUPCAKES
WITH DARK CHOCOLATE GLOSS

I love surprises and filled cupcakes can be such a pleasant one! Vanilla cake speckled with cacao nibs and filled with dark chocolate fudge—simply divine!

makes 24 mini cupcakes

CHOCOLATE CHIP CUPCAKES
1½ cups peeled and chopped apples
1½ teaspoons lemon juice
6 tablespoons raw honey or agave
¼ cup raw coconut oil
seeds of 1 vanilla bean
1 teaspoon organic vanilla extract
pinch of Himalayan salt
1 cup raw coconut flour
¼ cup cacao nibs

DARK CHOCOLATE GLOSS
⅔ cup raw agave nectar
6 tablespoons raw coconut oil
1 cup raw cacao powder

CHOCOLATE CHIP CUPCAKES   Place the chopped apples in your food processor fit with the S-blade and process until smooth. Immediately add the lemon juice and process to prevent browning. Add the honey, coconut oil, vanilla bean, vanilla extract & salt and process again until well combined. Add the coconut flour and process until completely combined. Finally, add the cacao nibs and pulse quickly to distribute. Fill mini cupcake liners with 1 heaping tablespoon of cake mixture. Press into the bottom and up the sides, leaving a ¾" deep thumbprint in the center. Place in the freezer to set for 1-2 hours. Once solid, pop the cupcakes out of the liners and they're ready to be filled & frosted.

DARK CHOCOLATE GLOSS   Whisk together all ingredients in a medium sized bowl until very smooth and shiny. When the cupcakes are set, fill the hole in the center and glaze the tops with the chocolate gloss. Place the cupcakes in the refrigerator for 1-2 hours to set the gloss.

Vanilla bean Cupcakes
with Lavender Blackberry Frosting

This is such an elegant combination. The sophisticated flavors of lavender and blackberries shine atop a classic vanilla cake. This is absolutely one of my all time favorites.

makes one dozen regular or 30 mini cupcakes

Vanilla Bean Cupcakes
3 cups peeled and chopped apples
1 tablespoon lemon juice
¾ cup raw honey or agave
½ cup raw coconut oil
seeds of 2 vanilla beans
2 teaspoons organic vanilla extract
pinch of Himalayan salt
2 cups raw coconut flour

Lavender Blackberry Frosting
¾ cup water
¾ cup coconut butter (not oil!)
seeds of 1 vanilla bean
½ cup raw honey or agave
1¼ cup raw macadamia nuts, soaked
    for 4 hours, drained/rinsed
2 teaspoons dried lavender
2 cups blackberries

Vanilla Bean Cupcakes Place the chopped apples in your food processor fit with the S-blade and process until smooth. Immediately add the lemon juice and process to prevent browning. Add the honey or agave, coconut oil, vanilla bean, vanilla extract & salt and process again until well combined. Finally, add the coconut flour and process until completely combined. Fill your cupcake liners to the top and press firmly to form their shape. Freeze for 2 hours to firm. Once solid, pop the cupcakes out of the liners and they're ready to be frosted.

Lavender Blackberry Frosting Place all ingredients except for the lavender and blackberries in a high-speed blender and blend from low to high. Once your cream is very smooth, add the lavender and blend gently until combined. Pour into a medium sized bowl. Place the blackberries in a separate bowl and mash with a fork until the juices are released and you are left with small pieces of fruit. Pour the berries and juice into the lavender cream and stir gently to swirl the colors. Refrigerate the frosting for 2-4 hours to firm. Once it has thickened, frost the cupcakes.

cupcake heaven.

BANANA WALNUT CUPCAKES
WITH SWEET CINNAMON FROSTING

Oh my! This cupcake is the most perfect raw food version of banana bread that I have ever experienced. Perfectly moist and cakey, with crunchy cinnamon walnuts and a sweet cinnamon cream equal a pleasure overload! If you're just in the mood for straight up banana bread, this is even amazing without the frosting.

makes one dozen regular or 30 mini cupcakes

BANANA WALNUT CUPCAKES
3½ cups chopped ripe bananas
¼ cup raw honey or agave
½ cup raw coconut oil
2 teaspoons organic vanilla extract
1½ teaspoons cinnamon
pinch of Himalayan salt
2 cups raw coconut flour
1 cup chopped walnuts
2 tablespoons raw honey or agave
2 teaspoons cinnamon
pinch of Himalayan salt

SWEET CINNAMON FROSTING
2½ cups raw cashews soaked for 2
    hours, drained/rinsed
½ cup raw honey or agave nectar
½ cup pure water
2 tablespoons lemon juice
1 tablespoon cinnamon
pinch of salt
⅔ cup raw coconut oil

BANANA WALNUT CUPCAKES   Place the chopped bananas in your food processor fit with the S-blade and process until smooth. Add ¼ cup of honey or agave, coconut oil, vanilla, 1½ teaspoons cinnamon & salt and process again until well combined. Finally, add the coconut flour and process until completely combined. Scrape into a large bowl. In a separate bowl, toss together the walnuts, 2 tablespoons of honey or agave, 2 teaspoons of cinnamon and salt. Mix very well to coat all of the walnuts. Scrape the walnuts into the bowl with the cake mixture. Mix well to distribute the walnuts evenly throughout the cake. Fill your cupcake liners to the top and press firmly to form their shape. Freeze for 2 hours to firm. Once solid, pop the cupcakes out of the liners and they're ready to be frosted.

SWEET CINNAMON FROSTING   Place the cashews, honey or agave, water, lemon, cinnamon and salt in a high-speed blender. Blend until very smooth. Add the coconut oil and blend again until just combined. Refrigerate the frosting for 2-4 hours to firm. Once it has thickened, frost the cupcakes.

DARK CHOCOLATE CUPCAKES
WITH MEXICAN CHOCOLATE FROSTING

These are so rich and decadent that I love making them into mini cupcakes. The chocolate cake is perfectly fluffy and the frosting has just the right amount of spice when you're in the mood for a more unique chocolate flavor.

makes one dozen regular or 30 mini cupcakes

DARK CHOCOLATE CUPCAKES
3 cups peeled and chopped apples
1 cup raw honey or agave
½ cup raw coconut oil
¼ cup pure water
1⅓ cups raw cacao powder
seeds of one vanilla bean
pinch of Himalayan salt
2 cups raw coconut flour

MEXICAN CHOCOLATE FROSTING
2 cups raw cashews, soaked 2 hours, drained/rinsed
¾ cup + 2 tablespoons raw cacao powder
¾ cup raw honey or agave
¾ cup pure water
½ cup melted raw cacao butter
2 vanilla beans
1 teaspoon cinnamon
¾ teaspoon chili powder
pinch of cayenne
pinch of Himalayan salt

DARK CHOCOLATE CUPCAKES Place the chopped apples in your food processor fit with the S-blade and process until smooth. Add the honey, coconut oil & water and process again until well combined. Add the cacao powder, vanilla and salt and continue to process. Finally, add the coconut flour and process until completely combined. Fill your cupcake liners to the top and press firmly to form their shape. Freeze for 2 hours to firm. Once solid, pop the cupcakes out of the liners and they're ready to be frosted.

MEXICAN CHOCOLATE FROSTING Place all ingredients in a high-powered blender and blend until very smooth. Place the frosting in the refrigerator for 2 hours to firm. Once it has thickened, frost the cupcakes.

STRAWBERRY CUPCAKES
WITH CITRUS MINT FROSTING

Strawberry was a favorite cake flavor for the KW kids as we were growing up. These are perfectly fruity in flavor and gorgeously pink in color. The frosting is the ideal complement with a beautiful blend of citrus zest and fresh mint.

makes one dozen regular or 30 mini cupcakes

STRAWBERRY CUPCAKES

2 cups chopped strawberries, packed
¾ cup raw honey or agave
½ cup raw coconut oil
seeds of 2 vanilla beans
pinch of Himalayan salt
2 cups raw coconut flour

CITRUS MINT FROSTING

2½ cups raw cashews, soaked for 2
    hours, drained/rinsed
½ cup raw honey or agave
6 tablespoons fresh orange juice
¼ cup pure water
1 teaspoon lemon zest
1 teaspoon orange zest
½ teaspoon lime zest
seeds of one vanilla bean
pinch of Himalayan salt
⅓ cup raw coconut oil
2 tablespoons chopped mint leaves

STRAWBERRY CUPCAKES Place the strawberries in your food processor fit with the S-blade and process until smooth. Add the honey or agave, coconut oil, vanilla bean & salt and process again until well combined. Finally, add the coconut flour and process until completely combined. Fill your cupcake liners to the top and press firmly to form their shape. Freeze for 2 hours to firm. Once solid, pop the cupcakes out of the liners and they're ready to be frosted.

CITRUS MINT FROSTING Place the cashews, honey or agave, orange juice, water, lemon zest, orange zest, lime zest, vanilla and salt in a high-speed blender. Blend until very smooth. Add the coconut oil and blend again until just combined. Finally, add the mint and blend lightly until the frosting is nicely speckled with green. Refrigerate the frosting for 2-4 hours to firm. Once it has thickened, frost the cupcakes.

Lemon Spiked Vanilla Cupcakes
with Sweet basil Frosting

When you're in the mood for a cupcake that's a bit more unique than your average vanilla or chocolate, this flavor is perfect. I love including surprises of fresh herbs in desserts when they may be least expected. These are absolutely delicious with a hint of citrus in the classic vanilla cupcake and a super creamy, sweet herb frosting.

makes one dozen regular or 30 mini cupcakes

Lemon Spiked Vanilla Cupcakes

3 cups peeled and chopped apples
1 tablespoon lemon juice
¾ cup raw honey or agave
½ cup raw coconut oil
seeds of 2 vanilla beans
2 teaspoons organic vanilla extract
1 teaspoon lemon zest
pinch of Himalayan salt
2 cups raw coconut flour

Sweet Basil Frosting

2½ cups raw cashews, soaked for 2
   hours, drained/rinsed
½ cup raw honey or agave
6 tablespoons lemon juice
¼ cup pure water
1 teaspoon lemon zest
seeds of one vanilla bean
pinch of Himalayan salt
⅓ cup raw coconut oil
¼ cup young basil leaves

Lemon Spiked Vanilla Cupcakes   Place the chopped apples in your food processor fit with the S-blade and process until smooth. Immediately add the lemon juice and process to prevent browning. Add the honey or agave, coconut oil, vanilla bean, vanilla extract, lemon zest & salt and process again until well combined. Finally, add the coconut flour and process until completely combined. Fill your cupcake liners to the top and press firmly to form their shape. Freeze for 2 hours to firm. Once solid, pop the cupcakes out of the liners and they're ready to be frosted.

Sweet Basil Frosting   Place the cashews, honey or agave, lemon, water, lemon zest, vanilla and salt in a high-speed blender. Blend until very smooth. Add the coconut oil and blend again until just combined. Finally, add the basil and blend lightly until the frosting is nicely speckled with green. Refrigerate the frosting for 2-4 hours to firm. Once it has thickened, frost the cupcakes.

Strawberry Cupcakes
with Honey Ginger Frosting

Sweet strawberries and spicy ginger are a luscious combination. If you have any frosting left over, it's so delicious as a dip for extra strawberries.

makes one dozen regular or 30 mini cupcakes

Strawberry Cupcakes
2 cups chopped strawberries, packed
¾ cup raw honey or agave
½ cup raw coconut oil
seeds of 2 vanilla beans
pinch of salt
2 cups raw coconut flour

Honey Ginger Frosting
2½ cups raw cashews, soaked for 2
   hours, drained/rinsed
½ cup raw honey
6 tablespoons lemon juice
¼ cup pure water
2 teaspoons grated fresh ginger
seeds of one vanilla bean
pinch of Himalayan salt
⅓ cup raw coconut oil

Strawberry Cupcakes Place the strawberries in your food processor fit with the S-blade and process until smooth. Add the honey or agave, coconut oil, vanilla bean & salt and process again until well combined. Finally, add the coconut flour and process until completely combined. Fill your cupcake liners to the top and press firmly to form their shape. Freeze for 2 hours to firm. Once solid, pop the cupcakes out of the liners and they're ready to be frosted.

Honey Ginger Frosting Place the cashews, honey, lemon juice, water, ginger, vanilla and salt in a high-speed blender. Blend until very smooth. Add the coconut oil and blend again until just combined. Refrigerate the frosting for 2-4 hours to firm. Once it has thickened, frost the cupcakes.

Dark Chocolate Cupcakes
with Mint Chip Frosting

Rich, fluffy chocolate cupcakes topped with a cool, mint whipped frosting is like marrying soul mates! I love the crunch that cacao nibs add to the smooth frosting—these are heavenly.

makes one dozen regular or 30 mini cupcakes

Dark Chocolate Cupcakes

3 cups peeled and chopped apples
1 cup raw honey or agave
½ cup raw coconut oil
¼ cup pure water
1⅓ cups raw cacao powder
seeds of one vanilla bean
pinch of Himalayan salt
2 cups raw coconut flour

Mint Chip Frosting

1½ cups raw cashews, soaked 2 hours, drained/rinsed
⅔ cup raw honey or raw agave
⅓ cup melted raw cacao butter
¼ cup pure water
¼ teaspoon peppermint extract
⅛ teaspoon spirulina (for color)
seeds of 1 vanilla bean
pinch of Himalayan salt
¼ cup raw cacao nibs

Dark Chocolate Cupcakes Place the chopped apples in your food processor fit with the S-blade and process until smooth. Add the honey or agave, coconut oil & water and process again until well combined. Add the cacao powder, vanilla & salt and continue to process. Finally, add the coconut flour and process until completely combined. Fill your cupcake liners to the top and press firmly to form their shape. Freeze for 2 hours to firm. Once solid, pop the cupcakes out of the liners and they're ready to be frosted.

Mint Chip Frosting Place all ingredients except for the cacao nibs in a high-powered blender and blend until very smooth. Scrape into a bowl and fold in the cacao nibs. Place the frosting in the refrigerator for 2 hours to firm. Once it has thickened, frost the cupcakes.

Vanilla Bean Cupcakes
with Peaches & Cream Frosting

This cupcake is perfect for peach season when you can get your hands on the freshest, juiciest ripe fruit.

makes one dozen regular or 30 mini cupcakes

Vanilla Bean Cupcakes
3 cups peeled and chopped apples
1 tablespoon lemon juice
¾ cup raw honey or agave
½ cup raw coconut oil
seeds of 2 vanilla beans
2 teaspoons organic vanilla extract
pinch of Himalayan salt
2 cups raw coconut flour

Peaches & Cream Frosting
1 cup raw coconut butter (not oil!)
1 cup chopped peaches
¼ cup raw honey or raw agave
¼ cup pure water
1 teaspoon organic vanilla extract
pinch of Himalayan salt
1 cup finely chopped peaches

Vanilla Bean Cupcakes Place the chopped apples in your food processor fit with the S-blade and process until smooth. Immediately add the lemon juice and process to prevent browning. Add the honey or agave, coconut oil, vanilla bean, vanilla extract & salt and process again until well combined. Finally, add the coconut flour and process until completely combined. Fill your cupcake liners to the top and press firmly to form their shape. Freeze for 2 hours to firm. Once solid, pop the cupcakes out of the liners and they're ready to be frosted.

Peaches & Cream Frosting In a high-speed blender, combine the coconut butter, 1 cup of peaches, honey or agave, water, vanilla & salt and blend until very smooth. Pour into a bowl and fold in the remaining chopped peaches. Set the frosting in the refrigerator for 1-2 hours to firm. Once it has thickened, frost the cupcakes. Be careful not to refrigerate for too long before frosting as the coconut butter will become stiff and difficult to spread.

VANILLA BEAN CUPCAKES
WITH RASPBERRY JAM & LEMON CREAM FROSTING

This is a very elegant cupcake with a luscious surprise of raspberry jam in the center. The creamy lemon frosting sweetly complements the fruity filling. These are best served with a sophisticated cup of tea on the side.

makes 15 regular cupcakes

VANILLA BEAN CUPCAKES

3 cups peeled and chopped apples
1 tablespoon lemon juice
¾ cup raw honey or agave
½ cup raw coconut oil
seeds of 2 vanilla beans
2 teaspoons organic vanilla extract
pinch of Himalayan salt
2 cups raw coconut flour

LEMON CREAM FROSTING

2½ cups raw cashews, soaked 2 hours, drained/rinsed
½ cup raw honey or raw agave
½ cup lemon juice
1 teaspoon lemon zest
⅛ teaspoon turmeric (optional for color)
pinch of salt
⅓ cup raw coconut oil

RASPBERRY JAM

2 cups raspberries
¼ cup raw honey or agave
¼ cup chia seed

VANILLA BEAN CUPCAKES Place the chopped apples in your food processor fit with the S-blade and process until smooth. Immediately add the lemon juice and process to prevent browning. Add the honey or agave, coconut oil, vanilla bean, vanilla extract & salt and process again until well combined. Finally, add the coconut flour and process until completely combined. Fill your cupcake liners to the top and press firmly to form their shape. Scoop out the center (about 1"x1") to make room for the filling. Freeze for 2 hours to firm. Once solid, pop the cupcakes out of the liners and they're ready to be filled & frosted.

RASPBERRY JAM In a blender, combine the raspberries and honey or agave. Blend lightly. Scrape into a bowl and fold in the chia seeds. Set aside to thicken for about 30 minutes. Once the jam has thickened, spoon into the hollow centers of your cupcakes.

LEMON CREAM FROSTING In a high-speed blender, combine the cashews, honey or agave, lemon juice, lemon zest, turmeric & salt and blend until very smooth. Add the coconut oil and blend again until just combined. Set the frosting in the refrigerator for 2-4 hours to firm. Once it has thickened, frost the cupcakes.

DARK CHOCOLATE CUPCAKES
WITH WHITE CHOCOLATE MACADAMIA FROSTING

White chocolate and macadamia nuts unite two of my favorite flavors. With them both resting on top of these fabulous chocolate cupcakes, we have reached a new level of sweet pleasure!

makes one dozen regular or 30 mini cupcakes

DARK CHOCOLATE CUPCAKES
3 cups peeled and chopped apples
1 cup raw honey or agave
½ cup raw coconut oil
¼ cup pure water
1⅓ cups raw cacao powder
seeds of one vanilla bean
pinch of Himalayan salt
2 cups raw coconut flour

WHITE CHOCOLATE MACADAMIA FROSTING
1½ cups raw macadamia nuts, soaked 4 hours, drained/rinsed
½ cup raw honey or raw agave
½ cup melted raw cacao butter
6 tablespoons pure water
seeds of 2 vanilla beans
pinch of Himalayan salt
½ cup chopped raw macadamia nuts

DARK CHOCOLATE CUPCAKES Place the chopped apples in your food processor fit with the S-blade and process until smooth. Add the honey, coconut oil & water and process again until well combined. Add the cacao powder, vanilla and salt and continue to process. Finally, add the coconut flour and process until completely combined. Fill your cupcake liners to the top and press firmly to form their shape. Freeze for 2 hours to firm. Once solid, pop the cupcakes out of the liners and they're ready to be frosted.

WHITE CHOCOLATE MACADAMIA FROSTING Place all ingredients except for the chopped macadamia nuts in a high-powered blender and blend until very smooth. Place the frosting in the refrigerator for 2 hours to firm. Once it has thickened, frost the cupcakes. Top each cupcake with a sprinkling of the chopped macadamia nuts.

Vanilla Orange Cupcakes
With Goji Cream Frosting

The color speaks volumes on this delicious cupcake—it's flavor is bright, bold & fun! Creamy vanilla and juicy oranges create the perfect cupcake flavor to accompany this exotic goji berry cream.

makes one dozen regular or 30 mini cupcakes

Vanilla Orange Cupcakes

2½ cups peeled and chopped apples
6 tablespoons fresh orange juice
¾ cup raw honey or agave
½ cup raw coconut oil
2 teaspoons organic vanilla extract
2 teaspoons orange zest
pinch of Himalayan salt
2 cups raw coconut flour

Goji Cream Frosting

1 cup fresh orange juice
6 tablespoons goji berries
2 cups raw cashews, soaked 2 hours,
  drained/rinsed
½ cup raw honey or agave
1 teaspoon vanilla extract
pinch of Himalayan salt
½ cup raw coconut oil

VANILLA ORANGE CUPCAKES   Place the chopped apples in your food processor fit with the S-blade and process until smooth. Immediately add the orange juice and process to prevent browning. Add the honey or agave, coconut oil, vanilla bean, vanilla extract, orange zest & salt and process again until well combined. Finally, add the coconut flour and process until completely combined. Fill your cupcake liners to the top and press firmly to form their shape. Freeze for 2 hours to firm. Once solid, pop the cupcakes out of the liners and they're ready to be frosted.

GOJI CREAM FROSTING   Soak the goji berries in the orange juice for one hour. In a high-speed blender, combine the soaked goji berries and the orange juice, cashews, honey or agave, vanilla & salt and blend until very smooth. Add the coconut oil and blend again until just combined. Set the frosting in the refrigerator for 2-4 hours to firm. Once it has thickened, frost the cupcakes.

DARK CHOCOLATE CUPCAKES
WITH JUICY RASPBERRY FROSTING

Fluffy chocolate cupcakes, vanilla cream and juicy raspberries come together in a divine union of tastes, textures and colors that are sure to please.

makes one dozen regular or 30 mini cupcakes

DARK CHOCOLATE CUPCAKES
3 cups peeled and chopped apples
1 cup raw honey or agave
½ cup raw coconut oil
¼ cup pure water
1⅓ cups raw cacao powder
seeds of one vanilla bean
pinch of Himalayan salt
2 cups raw coconut flour

JUICY RASPBERRY FROSTING
2½ cups raw cashews, soaked for 2
    hours, drained/rinsed
½ cup raw honey or agave
6 tablespoons lemon juice
¼ cup pure water
seeds of one vanilla bean
⅛ teaspoon Himalayan salt
⅓ cup raw coconut oil
1½ cups fresh raspberries

DARK CHOCOLATE CUPCAKES Place the chopped apples in your food processor fit with the S-blade and process until smooth. Add the honey, coconut oil & water and process again until well combined. Add the cacao powder, vanilla & salt and continue to process. Finally, add the coconut flour and process until completely combined. Fill your cupcake liners to the top and press firmly to form their shape. Freeze for 2 hours to firm. Once solid, pop the cupcakes out of the liners and they're ready to be frosted.

JUICY RASPBERRY FROSTING Place the cashews, honey or agave, lemon, water, vanilla and salt in a high-speed blender. Blend until very smooth. Add the coconut oil and blend again until just combined. Scrape into a medium bowl and fold in the raspberries. Mix well to gently crush the berries and swirl the colors. Refrigerate the frosting for 2-4 hours to firm. Once it has thickened, frost the cupcakes.

Vanilla Bean Cupcakes
With Chocolate Chip Frosting

This is a favorite among my friends and the first to go at a cupcake party. Yes, I host those!

makes one dozen regular or 30 mini cupcakes

Vanilla Bean Cupcakes
3 cups peeled and chopped apples
1 tablespoon lemon juice
¾ cup raw honey or agave
½ cup raw coconut oil
seeds of 2 vanilla beans
2 teaspoons organic vanilla extract
pinch of Himalayan salt
2 cups raw coconut flour

Chocolate Chip Frosting
2 cups raw cashews, soaked 2 hours,
   drained/rinsed
¾ cup raw honey or agave
⅔ cup melted raw cacao butter
6 tablespoons pure water
seeds of 2 vanilla beans
generous pinch of Himalayan salt
¼ cup cacao nibs

VANILLA BEAN CUPCAKES Place the chopped apples in your food processor fit with the S-blade and process until smooth. Immediately add the lemon juice and process to prevent browning. Add the honey or agave, coconut oil, vanilla bean, vanilla extract & salt and process again until well combined. Finally, add the coconut flour and process until completely combined. Fill your cupcake liners to the top and press firmly to form their shape. Freeze for 2 hours to firm. Once solid, pop the cupcakes out of the liners and they're ready to be frosted.

CHOCOLATE CHIP FROSTING In a high-speed blender, combine the cashews, honey or agave, cacao butter, water, vanilla & salt and blend until very smooth. Pour into a bowl and fold in the cacao nibs. Set the frosting in the refrigerator for 2 hours to firm. Once it has thickened, frost the cupcakes.

CARROT GOJI CUPCAKES
WITH CREAM CHEESE FROSTING

This is a perfectly fluffy carrot cake speckled with bright red goji berries and spread with a generous helping of classic cream cheese frosting. This recipe is an ode to my first coconut flour cake discovery!

makes 10 regular cupcakes

CARROT GOJI CUPCAKES

3 cups chopped carrots
   (about 8 medium carrots)
½ cup raw honey or agave
½ cup raw coconut oil
1½ tablespoons cinnamon
1 teaspoon vanilla extract
1 teaspoon grated fresh ginger
¼ teaspoon nutmeg
pinch of Himalayan salt
1 cup raw coconut flour
¼ cup goji berries

CREAM CHEESE FROSTING

2½ cups raw cashews, soaked for 2
   hours, drained/rinsed
½ cup raw honey or agave
6 tablespoons lemon juice
¼ cup pure water
seeds of one vanilla bean
⅛ teaspoon Himalayan salt
⅓ cup raw coconut oil

CARROT GOJI CUPCAKES Place the chopped carrots in your food processor fit with the S-blade and process until smooth. Add the honey or agave, coconut oil, cinnamon, vanilla, ginger, nutmeg & salt and process again until well combined. Finally, add the coconut flour and process until completely combined. Scrape into a large bowl and fold in the goji berries. Mix well to evenly distribute the berries. Fill your cupcake liners to the top and press firmly to form their shape. Freeze for 2 hours to firm. Once solid, pop the cupcakes out of the liners and they're ready to be frosted.

CREAM CHEESE FROSTING Place the cashews, honey or agave, lemon, water, vanilla and salt in a high-speed blender. Blend until very smooth. Add the coconut oil and blend again until just combined. Refrigerate the frosting for 2-4 hours to firm. Once it has thickened, frost the cupcakes.

Vanilla Bean Cupcakes
With White Chocolate Rose Frosting

This is a gorgeous cupcake made extra special with a lovely white chocolate and rose petal frosting.

makes one dozen regular or 30 mini cupcakes

Vanilla Bean Cupcakes

3 cups peeled and chopped apples
1 tablespoon lemon juice
¾ cup raw honey or agave
½ cup raw coconut oil
seeds of 2 vanilla beans
2 teaspoons organic vanilla extract
pinch of Himalayan salt
2 cups raw coconut flour

White Chocolate Rose Frosting

½ cup water
1 tablespoon dried organic rose petals
2 cups raw cashews, soaked 2 hours, drained/rinsed
¾ cup raw honey or raw agave
⅔ cup melted raw cacao butter
seeds of 2 vanilla beans
pinch of Himalayan salt
6 tablespoons dried organic rose petals
1 teaspoon beet juice (for color)

Vanilla Bean Cupcakes Place the chopped apples in your food processor fit with the S-blade and process until smooth. Immediately add the lemon juice and process to prevent browning. Add the honey or agave, coconut oil, vanilla bean, vanilla extract & salt and process again until well combined. Finally, add the coconut flour and process until completely combined. Fill your cupcake liners to the top and press firmly to form their shape. Freeze for 2 hours to firm. Once solid, pop the cupcakes out of the liners and they're ready to be frosted.

White Chocolate Rose Frosting Heat the water in a tea kettle on the stove top. Once hot, pour over the 1 tablespoon of rose petals and let steep for 5 minutes to make rose tea. Strain and allow to cool. In a high-speed blender, combine the rose tea, cashews, honey or agave, cacao butter, vanilla & salt and blend until very smooth. Add the additional rose petals and beet juice and blend again until well combined. Set the frosting in the refrigerator for 2 hours to firm. Once it has thickened, frost the cupcakes.

ALMOND CUPCAKES
WITH CHOCOLATE ALMOND FROSTING

I think this must be my favorite cupcake of the whole book—if I have to choose just one. Light, fluffy almond cake topped with thick, rich chocolate almond frosting instantly transports me to cupcake heaven!

makes one dozen regular or 30 mini cupcakes

ALMOND CUPCAKES
3 cups peeled and chopped apples
¾ cup raw honey or agave
½ cup cold-pressed coconut oil
1½ teaspoons almond extract
pinch of Himalayan salt
2 cups raw coconut flour

CHOCOLATE ALMOND FROSTING
2 cups raw cashews, soaked 2 hours, drained/rinsed
¾ cup + 2 tablespoons raw cacao powder
¾ cup raw honey or raw agave
¾ cup pure water
½ cup melted raw cacao butter
1 teaspoon almond extract
pinch of Himalayan salt

ALMOND CUPCAKES Place the chopped apples in your food processor fit with the S-blade and process until smooth. Add the honey or agave, coconut oil, almond extract & salt and process again until well combined. Finally, add the coconut flour and process until completely combined. Fill your cupcake liners to the top and press firmly to form their shape. Freeze for 2 hours to firm. Once solid, pop the cupcakes out of the liners and they're ready to be frosted.

CHOCOLATE ALMOND FROSTING In a high-speed blender, combine the cashews, cacao powder, honey or agave, water, cacao butter, almond extract & salt and blend until very smooth. Set the frosting in the refrigerator for 2 hours to firm. Once it has thickened, frost the cupcakes.

BLUEBERRY CUPCAKES
WITH CINNAMON CRUMBLE

In the summer, I always have a blueberry muffin craving. This must stem from memories of foraging wild blueberries and baking with my mom. These are the absolute perfect answer to my desire.

makes 48 mini cupcakes

BLUEBERRY CUPCAKES
3 cups peeled and chopped apples
¼ cup lemon juice
¾ cup raw honey or agave
½ cup raw coconut oil
2 teaspoons organic vanilla extract
2 teaspoon lemon zest
¼ teaspoon nutmeg
pinch of Himalayan salt
2 cups raw coconut flour
¾ cup dried blueberries

CINNAMON CRUMBLE
3 cups shredded coconut
¼ cup raw honey or agave
¼ cup raw coconut oil
4 teaspoons cinnamon
½ teaspoon nutmeg
seeds of 1 vanilla bean
pinch of Himalayan salt

BLUEBERRY CUPCAKES Place the chopped apples in your food processor fit with the S-blade and process until smooth. Immediately add the lemon juice and process to prevent browning. Add the honey or agave, coconut oil, vanilla extract, lemon zest, nutmeg & salt and process again until well combined. Finally, add the coconut flour and process until completely combined. Scrape into a large bowl and fold in the dried blueberries. Fill your cupcake liners, leaving ¼" of space at the top and press firmly to form their shape.

CINNAMON CRUMBLE Place all ingredients in your food processor fit with the S-blade. Pulse to combine into a crumbly mixture. Divide equally among your cupcakes and press into the tops of each. Freeze 2 hours to firm. Once firm, pop the cupcakes out of their liners.

LEMON POPPY SEED CUPCAKES
WITH TART LEMON FROSTING

My grandmother always baked the most delicious, love-filled, lemon poppy seed cake, drizzled with a light lemon icing. This is my version, filled with just as much love!

makes one dozen regular or 30 mini cupcakes

LEMON POPPY SEED CUPCAKES

2½ cups peeled and chopped apples
1 cup raw honey or agave
½ cup lemon juice
½ cup raw coconut oil
3 teaspoons lemon zest
¼ teaspoon turmeric (for color)
pinch of Himalayan salt
2 cups raw coconut flour
3 tablespoons poppy seed

TART LEMON FROSTING

1 cup raw cashews, soaked 2 hours, drained/rinsed
½ cup pure water
½ cup lemon juice
1 teaspoon lemon zest
¼ cup honey or agave
pinch of salt
½ cup raw coconut oil

LEMON POPPY SEED CUPCAKES Place the chopped apples in your food processor fit with the S-blade and process until smooth. Immediately add the lemon juice and process to prevent browning. Add the honey or agave, coconut oil, vanilla extract, lemon zest, turmeric & salt and process again until well combined. Finally, add the coconut flour and process until completely combined. Scrape into a large bowl and fold in the poppy seed. Fill your cupcake liners to the top and press firmly to form their shape. Freeze for 2 hours to firm. Once solid, pop the cupcakes out of the liners and they're ready to be frosted.

TART LEMON FROSTING Place the cashews, water, lemon juice, lemon zest, honey or agave and salt in a high-speed blender. Blend until very smooth. Add the coconut oil and blend again until just combined. Refrigerate the frosting for 2-4 hours to firm. Once it has thickened, frost the cupcakes.

DARK CHOCOLATE CUPCAKES
WITH BUTTER PECAN FROSTING

By now, I'm sure you've fallen in love with the chocolate cupcake. Topped here with a fluffy, buttery frosting and rich, sticky pecan topping, this is another divine delight.

makes one dozen regular or 30 mini cupcakes

DARK CHOCOLATE CUPCAKES
3 cups peeled and chopped apples
1 cup raw honey or agave
½ cup raw coconut oil
¼ cup pure water
1⅓ cups raw cacao powder
seeds of one vanilla bean
pinch of Himalayan salt
2 cups raw coconut flour

BUTTER PECAN FROSTING
2 cups raw pecans, soaked 4-6 hours, drained/rinsed
¾ cup pure water
½ cup raw honey or agave
1 teaspoon organic vanilla extract
¼ teaspoon salt
½ cup raw coconut oil

BUTTER PECAN TOPPING
¼ cup raw honey or agave
½ teaspoon organic vanilla extract
pinch of salt
1 cup roughly chopped raw pecans

DARK CHOCOLATE CUPCAKES Place the chopped apples in your food processor fit with the S-blade and process until smooth. Add the honey, coconut oil & water and process again until well combined. Add the cacao powder, vanilla and salt and continue to process. Finally, add the coconut flour and process until completely combined. Fill your cupcake liners to the top and press firmly to form their shape. Freeze for 2 hours to firm. Once solid, pop the cupcakes out of the liners and they're ready to be frosted.

BUTTER PECAN FROSTING Place the pecans, water, honey or agave, vanilla and salt in a high-powered blender and blend until very smooth. Add the coconut oil and blend again until just combined. Refrigerate the frosting for 2-4 hours to firm. Once it has thickened, frost the cupcakes.

BUTTER PECAN TOPPING In a medium bowl, whisk together the honey or agave, vanilla and salt. Add in the pecans and stir to coat. Divide equally by placing a bit on top of each frosted cupcake.

BLACK FOREST CUPCAKES

When cherries are at their seasonal peak, what better way to use them than hiding inside of a chocolate cupcake and topped with vanilla cream.

makes 15 regular cupcakes

DARK CHOCOLATE CUPCAKES
3 cups peeled and chopped apples
1 cup raw honey or agave
½ cup raw coconut oil
¼ cup pure water
1⅓ cups raw cacao powder
seeds of one vanilla bean
pinch of Himalayan salt
2 cups raw coconut flour

JUICY CHERRY FILLING
2½ cups pitted cherries
3 tablespoons honey or agave
¼ teaspoon almond extract

VANILLA FROSTING
¾ cup water
¼ cup Brazil Nuts
2 cups raw cashews, soaked 2 hours, drained/rinsed
½ cup raw honey or raw agave
⅔ cup raw coconut oil
seeds of 2 vanilla beans
2 teaspoons organic vanilla extract
generous pinch of Himalayan salt

DARK CHOCOLATE CUPCAKES Place the chopped apples in your food processor fit with the S-blade and process until smooth. Add the honey, coconut oil & water and process again until well combined. Add the cacao powder, vanilla and salt and continue to process. Finally, add the coconut flour and process until completely combined. Fill your cupcake liners to the top and press firmly to form their shape. Scoop out the center (about 1"x1") to make room for the filling. Freeze for 2 hours to firm. Once solid, pop the cupcakes out of the liners and they're ready to be filled & frosted.

JUICY CHERRY FILLING Place all ingredients in your food processor and pulse to roughly chop. Let stand for 15 minutes, then strain out the juice. Divide equally between your cupcakes, filling the centers.

VANILLA FROSTING Place the water and the Brazil nuts in a blender and blend until smooth. Using a nut milk bag, strain out the nut pulp to make Brazil Nut milk. Place the Brazil nut milk and the remaining ingredients in a high-speed blender and blend until very smooth. Place the frosting in the refrigerator for 2-4 hours to firm. Once it has thickened, frost the cupcakes.

GOLDEN BERRY CUPCAKES
WITH ORANGE CREAM FROSTING

Golden berries are one of my favorite dried fruits—tart, tangy and deliciously chewy. If you don't have them on hand, you can substitute dried cranberries for the same sweet & sour result.

makes one dozen regular or 30 mini cupcakes

GOLDEN BERRY CUPCAKES

3 cups peeled and chopped apples
1 tablespoon lemon juice
¾ cup raw honey or agave
½ cup raw coconut oil
seeds of 2 vanilla beans
2 teaspoons organic vanilla extract
pinch of Himalayan salt
2 cups raw coconut flour
⅔ cup dried golden berries

ORANGE CREAM FROSTING

2½ cups raw cashews, soaked 2 hours, drained/rinsed
¾ cup fresh orange juice
½ cup raw honey or agave
1 teaspoon organic vanilla extract
1 teaspoon orange zest
pinch of Himalayan salt
⅔ cup raw coconut oil

GOLDEN BERRY CUPCAKES Place the chopped apples in your food processor fit with the S-blade and process until smooth. Immediately add the lemon juice and process to prevent browning. Add the honey or agave, coconut oil, vanilla bean, vanilla extract & salt and process again until well combined. Finally, add the coconut flour and process until completely combined. Scrape into a bowl and fold in the golden berries. Fill your cupcake liners to the top and press firmly to form their shape. Freeze for 2 hours to firm. Once solid, pop the cupcakes out of the liners and they're ready to be frosted.

ORANGE CREAM FROSTING Place the cashews, orange juice, honey or agave, vanilla, orange zest and salt in a high-speed blender. Blend until very smooth. Add the coconut oil and blend again until just combined. Refrigerate the frosting for 2-4 hours to firm. Once it has thickened, frost the cupcakes.

VANILLA BEAN CUPCAKES
WITH MANGO & CARDAMOM FROSTING

Like an Indian lassi, I've always loved the flavors of mango and cardamom together. A cupcake that marries the two seems only natural.

makes 15 regular cupcakes

VANILLA BEAN CUPCAKES
3 cups peeled and chopped apples
1 tablespoon lemon juice
¾ cup raw honey or agave
½ cup raw coconut oil
seeds of 2 vanilla beans
2 teaspoons organic vanilla extract
pinch of Himalayan salt
2 cups raw coconut flour

CARDAMOM FROSTING
2½ cups raw cashews soaked 2 hours, drained/rinsed
½ cup raw honey or agave
½ cup pure water
2 teaspoons organic vanilla extract
½ teaspoon cardamom
pinch of salt
½ cup raw coconut oil

MANGO FILLING
2 cups diced mango
2 tablespoons raw honey or agave

VANILLA BEAN CUPCAKES Place the chopped apples in your food processor fit with the S-blade and process until smooth. Immediately add the lemon juice and process to prevent browning. Add the honey or agave, coconut oil, vanilla bean, vanilla extract & salt and process again until well combined. Finally, add the coconut flour and process until completely combined. Fill your cupcake liners to the top and press firmly to form their shape. Scoop out the center (about 1"x1") to make room for the filling. Freeze for 2 hours to firm. Once solid, pop the cupcakes out of the liners and they're ready to be filled & frosted.

MANGO FILLING Place all ingredients in a high-speed blender. Blend until very smooth. Divide equally among your cupcakes, spooning the filling into the center of the cupcakes. If you have any remaining filling, you can use it to decorate the tops of the cupcakes.

CARDAMOM FROSTING Place the cashews, honey or agave, water, vanilla, cardamom and salt in a high-speed blender. Blend until very smooth. Add the coconut oil and blend again until just combined. Refrigerate the frosting for 2-4 hours to firm. Once it has thickened, frost the cupcakes.

RESOURCES

Here is where you can find everything you need for your journey into cupcake heaven.

EARTH CIRCLE ORGANICS
1.877.922.FOOD
www.earthcircleorganics.com

Earth Circle Organics offers amazing raw food products like really raw cashews and cacao to wholesale customers. They are very connected with their suppliers and are standing by every product with the utmost integrity.

FRONTIER NATURAL PRODUCTS CO-OP
1.800.669.3275
www.frontiercoop.com

Frontier carries natural and organic herbs, spices, teas and flavoring extracts.

MOUNTAIN ROSE HERBS
1.800.879.3337
www.mountainroseherbs.com

Mountain Rose Herbs offers a full catalog of certified organic and sustainable herbs, spices, teas, essential oils and more.

NATURAL ZING
1.888.729.9464
www.naturalzing.com

Natural Zing is the largest raw vegan food distributor in the US offering over 1,500 products to consumers, natural food stores, restaurants, and raw food manufacturers. They carry everything you need to stock your raw pantry, including coconut flour.

ULTIMATE SUPERFOODS
1.800.728.2066
www.ultimatesuperfoods.com

Ultimate Superfoods carries my favorite clear, raw agave, superfood powders, vanilla beans and lots more goodness.

GRATITUDE

I'm forever grateful to my family & friends for supporting my vision, my work & my dreams.

To Adam, thank you for your constant love, support and devotion to me and my work and for being the funniest person that I have ever met.

To my Mom, Dad, Justin, Ian, Robin and Baba, thank you for sharing birthday cakes with me that inspired the importance of creating cakes & cupcakes in line with my lifestyle. There should never be a cake-less birthday!

To the Mills family, thank you for introducing me to my first vegan chocolate cake many years ago.

To my recipe testers: Wendy, Ishvara & Joy, thank you for your praise and feedback during the creative process.

To Pam & Tolisa, thank you for saving me & helping to finish these recipes the week before I moved!

To my digital goddesses, Cylleria, Jaszy, Jerah, Liz, Stina & Trista, thank you for the fun, advice, support and for the cupcake photo shoot!

To Melissa, thank you stepping into my life at the perfect moment.

To YOU, thank you for purchasing my books--I am beyond grateful to do what I love and share with people who appreciate my work.

Natalia